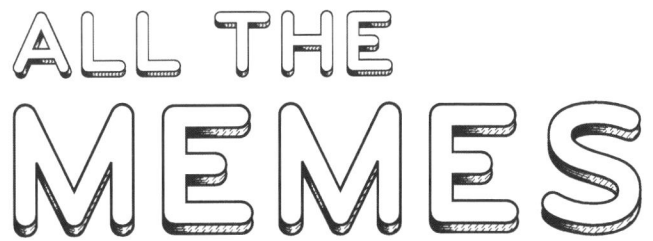

D1783679

# ALL THE MEMES

**An Epic Adult Coloring Book**

By D.B. Willaker

Available from Amazon.com and other retail outlets.

ISBN-13: 978-1533090454
ISBN-10: 1533090459

# COLOR TEST PAGE

Y U NO COLOR
ON IPHONE

*Evercolor*™

MEMES
FUNNY SAYINGS
SONG LYRICS

FREE

Download on the
App Store

www.evercolor.me

# COLOR TEST PAGE

## Y U NO COLOR ON IPHONE

*Evercolor*™

**MEMES**
**FUNNY SAYINGS**
**SONG LYRICS**

**FREE**

Download on the
**App Store**

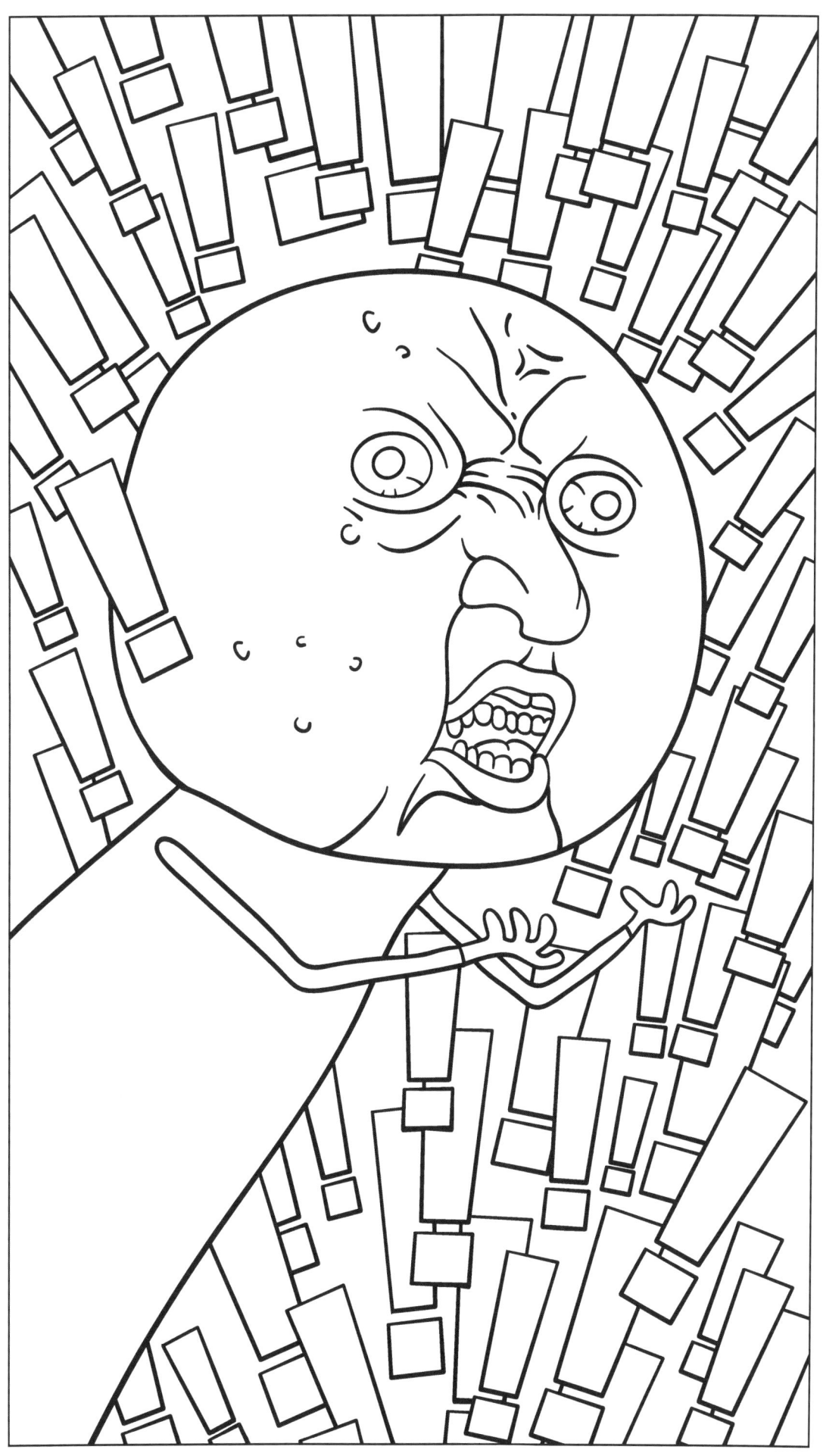

Printed in Poland
by Amazon Fulfillment
Poland Sp. z o.o., Wrocław